COVENANT • BIBLE • STUDIES

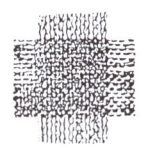

Voices in the Book of Job

Robert W. Neff

Study questions contributed by
Frank Ramirez

faithQuest® ♦ Brethren Press®

Voices in the Book of Job
Covenant Bible Studies Series

Copyright © 2005 by *faithQuest*®. Published by Brethren Press®, 1451 Dundee Avenue, Elgin, IL 60120.

All rights reserved. No portion of this book may be reproduced in any form or by any process or technique without the written consent of the publisher, except for brief quotations embodied in critical articles or reviews.

Unless otherwise noted, scripture quotations are from the New Revised Standard Version of the Bible, copyrighted 1989 by the National Council of Churches of Christ in the USA, Division of Education and Ministry.

Cover photo: Nick Yee

09 08 07 06 05   5 4 3 2 1

Library of Congress Control Number: 2005933970
ISBN-13: 978-0-87178-070-6
ISBN-10: 0-87178-070-4

Manufactured in the United States of America

Contents

Foreword vii
Preface ix
1. On Reading the Book of Job 1
2. The Wager Between God and the Accuser 9
3. The Voice of Traditional Piety 17
4. The Voice of a Caring Spouse 23
5. The Voice of Lament 29
6. The Voice of Traditional Wisdom 37
7. The Voice of Angry Complaint 43
8. The Voice of Judicial Integrity 51
9. The Voice of Creative Presence 59
10. The Voice of Renewed Life 65
Bibliography 71

Foreword

The Covenant Bible Studies series provides relational Bible studies for people who want to study the Bible in small groups rather than alone.

Relational Bible study is marked by certain characteristics that differ from other types of Bible study. We are reminded that relational Bible study is anchored in covenantal history. God covenanted with people in Old Testament history, established a new covenant in Jesus Christ, and covenants with the church today. Thus, this Bible study is intended for small groups of people who can meet face-to-face on a regular basis and share frankly and covenant with one another in an intimate group.

Relational Bible study takes seriously a corporate faith. As each person contributes to study, prayer, and work, the group becomes the real body of Christ. Each one's contribution is needed and important. "For just as the body in one and has many members, and all the members of the body, though many, are one body, so it is with Christ. . . . Now you are the body of Christ and individually members of it" (1 Cor. 12:12, 17).

Relational Bible study helps both individuals and the group to claim the promise of the Spirit and the working of the Spirit. As one person testified, "In our commitment to one another and in our sharing, something happened. . . . we were woven together in love by the Master Weaver. It is something that can happen only when two or three or seven are gathered in God's name and we know the promise of God's presence in our lives.

In the small group environment, the members aid one another in seeking to become

- biblically informed so they better understand the revelation of God;

- globally aware so they know themselves to be better connected with all of God's world;
- relationally sensitive to God, self, and others.

For people who choose to use this study in a small group, the following intentions will help create an atmosphere in which support will grow and faith will deepen.

1. As a small group of learners, we gather around God's word to discern its meaning for today.
2. The words, stories, and admonitions we find in scripture come alive for today, challenging and renewing us.
3. All people are learners and all are leaders.
4. Each person will contribute to the study, sharing the meaning found in the scripture and helping to bring meaning to others.
5. We recognize each other's vulnerability as we share out of our own experience, and in sharing we learn to trust others and to be trustworthy.

The questions in the Suggestions for Sharing and Prayer section are intended for use in the hour preceding the Bible study to foster intimacy in the covenant group and to relate personal sharing to the Bible study topic, preparing one another to go out again in all directions to be in the world.

Welcome to this study. As you search the scriptures, may you also search yourself. May God's voice and guidance and the love and encouragement of brothers and sisters in Christ challenge you to live more fully the abundant life God promises.

Preface

The Book of Job deals with many serious faith questions from several points of view: How shall I speak with God and friends about my faith? Is it okay to express anger and doubt in prayer? How do I understand suffering and my response to it? Do I serve God because of what God can do for me or because I love God without thought of reward? What is the source of evil? How do I define devotion and piety?

The Book of Job describes the faith journey of one human being who discovers a variety of responses to his circumstance of loss and suffering—responses within himself and from others, including the voice of God. These perspectives form the focus of this study and guide the development of the chapters in this work. I have referred to these perspectives simply as voices since they are presented in speeches throughout the Book of Job.

What are these voices? Through the course of the book, Job has a number of different voices: the confessions of a pious man (Job 1–2); the ravings of someone near death (Job 3); the complaints of an angry man (Job 6–7); the inquiring voice of a courtroom plaintiff (Job 29–31); and the voice of renewed life (Job 42). In addition to the voice of Job, there are the voices of the three friends: Eliphaz, Bildad, Zophar, and a young bystander, Elihu. Since the friends present variations in the position of traditional wisdom, I have selected the voice of Eliphaz in his strongest and most sympathetic speech (Job 4–5) to represent all of them. Job's spouse, on the other hand, has only one verse to her credit (Job 2:9), but her response to Job's suffering may enable Job to confront the crisis of loss in a different way from that of traditional piety. The speech of God from the whirlwind (Job 38–41) is by far the most powerful and brings Job to a new place in his life. However, it is the most debated in regard to the nature of God and creation. While this study does not require the complete reading of the Book of Job, it does require a careful reading of each of the assigned chapters in order to hear the voice under discussion. I have tried to provide a setting in which each voice will receive a sympathetic hearing and in such a way that the reader does not disregard anyone.

Some of us have spoken with different voices over our lifetime. Others have held the same voice throughout their faith journey. I have discovered that my faith life is enriched when I give a fair hearing to others. In fact, I confess that I read Job differently at this point in my life because of a study group that discussed many of the chapters I have presented here. Actually, if it were not for Frank Ramirez, who made me sit down and start writing some of the ideas that I shared, I would never have written this book. I thank him for his brotherly guidance. It is my hope that you will find the same joy in your study partners and that God may bless you in your reading and relating to the life of devotion as found in the Book of Job.

1

On Reading the Book of Job

Personal Preparation
1. Although this study does not require a reading of the entire Book of Job, one of the longer books of the Bible, you will benefit from doing so. You will notice that the first two chapters and much of the final chapter are written in story form, and that the rest is printed as poetry. Translating poetry can be difficult because poets intentionally use words that carry more than one meaning and images that are meant to convey meanings both through words and beyond the words. It's a good idea to read from more than one translation, particularly a modern English translation or study Bible, especially if you encounter a sentence or phrase that is difficult to understand.
2. You may find it helpful to have a notebook or journal handy for your preparation time each week.
3. Who is Job? Before you begin reading, write two or three sentences in your journal telling what you know, or think you know, about him.
4. Before the session, read the Understanding in this study guide. Consider the following question for the Discussion and Action portion of your meeting: What, if any, are the differences between story and history?
5. If you know in advance those who will be in your group and who will be leading the group, take time to pray for each person individually and for your learning together.

Suggestions for Sharing and Prayer

- As you gather for the first time, introduce yourselves by giving your name and a significant personal fact. After the first round of introductions, once more share simple greetings, i.e., "Hello to you all," this time using a different voice. For instance, one might give greetings in a friendly, suspicious, silly, or serious voice, and so on.
- Job is described in the Bible as a person beyond reproach. Spend some time naming people you know personally or by reputation who are like Job? What triumphs or tragedies have been part of that person's life? How do you perceive that these people have dealt with such events?
- In the Book of Job, God speaks in different voices and is addressed in different voices. How do group members address God, and under what circumstances? What are the appropriate ways, in their opinion, for God to be addressed?
- Spend some time in prayer, with group members addressing God in the following voices: a prayer of praise, a prayer of petition, and a prayer of promise. Conclude by selecting a hymn that speaks directly to God in prayer, e.g., "Eternal Spirit of the living Christ," "Holy Spirit, come with power."

Understanding

As I reflect on my life, I discover that my religious journey is lived between lament and praise, between outburst and quiet reflection, between joy and anger, and between devotion and doubt. For this reason I have spent a lifetime on the Book of Job, which parallels my own life experience without the extremity of loss. However, as I write, I am aware of the tragic loss of life without reason in Iraq, New York City, London, Madrid, and Israel/Palestine, as well as the loss of life and unimaginable destruction wreaked by Hurricane Katrina along the Gulf Coast and the tsunami in Southeast Asia. How shall we live in the context of loss without reason and the death of innocents?

Singer or Sage?

As we study Job, we will want to remember that this book straddles the traditions of explosive expression of song and dance (Psalms) and the sober and restrained reflection of scholars (Proverbs). As we shall see, Singer and Sage remain in tension in this book. In our Protestant Bibles, Job precedes Psalms, but in the Hebrew Bible, the Book of Job appears between Psalms (the hymn book of Israel) and Proverbs (the wisdom of the sages) and serves as a bridge between these two significant traditions.

The Book of Job has often been classified as a wisdom book. The sage reflects upon the nature and order of creation that has a coherence, reliability, and regularity. This tradition resides not only in Israel but throughout the Middle East from Egypt to Babylon. Thus, the reader should not be surprised that the names of the participants in this book suggest a tradition outside the boundaries of Israel. For example, international diplomats, courtiers, and managers were trained in schools that prepared young men to compete in the larger world of nations. In this tradition young men were trained to present argument, to maintain composure, and to use the power of language in the conduct of business. This position is found in the friends of Job who give a classic portrayal of wisdom teaching.

On the other hand, in many of the speeches of Job, we find the traditions and expressions of the lament Psalms. One of the leading experts on the liturgical tradition of Israel, Claus Westermann, maintains that the cries of the dispossessed and the afflicted, as found in Psalms 6; 22; and 88, to mention a few, appear in the speeches of Job. The individual in these psalms is distressed about life, angry with God, and explodes without contrition about the circumstances of this world. Clearly this is not the language of the first two chapters, but it is the language of Job in the larger portion of the book. This language is disturbing to the sage and violates the training of the wise, who believe that one should control his or her emotions at all times.

We in the community of faith are often uncomfortable with outbursts and outrageous language such as "My God, my God, why have you deserted me?" We want people to tone down insults and to refrain from lashing out at God. Yet these ravings find a home in much of the Psalter, in the complaints of Jeremiah (Jer. 11:18–12:6; 20:14-18), and in Job 3ff. Job's speeches are the lament of an individual who has lost everything from family and possessions to his health. Job goes beyond the sensibilities of our views of piety but expresses one consistent with much of the Psalms.

What we find then in this book is a clash of traditions on how to view and live in this world, each of which has been accepted in the canonical presentation of the faith. Far from finding one voice in this book, we may find two, three, or many more, and all have standing within the context of faith. Thus, one of the questions that may remain after our study is, Can we speak with one voice or with many in the household of faith?

History or Parable?
Another question to ask about the Book of Job: Should we think of this account of Job as history or parable? Since in our English versions of the Bible Job immediately follows the historical books and precedes Psalms, there is a strong inclination to interpret the book from an historical perspective. Clearly, the figure of Job is known from other texts in the Old Testament, which could mean that the book is about a righteous man who lived at one time. However, there is compelling reason for treating the story as a parable.

The Book of Job begins as an isolated chapter in the history of humankind. Unlike all other historical books in the Old Testament, there is no connection between the hero and Israel. He simply lives in the East where the locus of the book occurs. Most historical books in the Old Testament begin with the phrase "and there was," connecting the story with what preceded. There is no such connecting link in the Book of Job. He pops up from nowhere, as captured in the phrase "there was a man . . . ," without definitive linkage or direct tie to the past. What makes him important to us lies outside history and genealogy.

Because of the absence of genealogy and a precise location for the dwelling of Job, early Jewish commentators believed that this individual stood outside history. They thought that the whole story was a *mashal*, a parable about righteous suffering. The Babylonian Talmud asserted most directly, "Job did not exist." Some traditions, namely the Septuagint, the Greek version of the Old Testament, attempted to provide detail absent in the Hebrew text, presumably to make it seem more historical. Thus, the translators added an appendix at the end of the book to satisfy "historical curiosity."

The reader is told four pertinent details about Job's life: his homeland, his name, his family and possessions, and his relationship with God. He lives in the land of Uz. His name is Job. He is wealthy and prosperous with a perfect family and has the leading reputation in the region. These details are told only once. However, the fourth detail is stated three times in exactly the same way: "the man was blameless and upright, one who feared God and turned away from evil" (Job 1:1; 1:8; and 2:3). This description of Job is known in heaven and on earth, and the whole book depends upon this premise. For us, the readers, the birthplace and genealogy are not important because the story tells of the relationship of a human with God outside any historical context. In this sense the reader is free to think about the nature of piety, the inner life of an individual before God. The description of the character, devotion, and struggle of Job receives the greater attention. In this sense the story could happen at any time and at any place. It could be our story as well.

The reader now has the basis on which the whole book depends: a righteous man suffers. The reader needs to know and remember this fact as he or she proceeds through the book. We, the readers, unlike the friends, know specifically that Job is an innocent man, suffering through no fault of his own. In fact, we observe a human being who is the paradigm of right living, suffering indescribable loss and unspeakable anguish. The prologue provides the premise on which all else follows: Job—a man of integrity, upright, fearing God, and turning away from evil—suffers great wrong and unjust treatment.

Whether one reads the story as parable or history, what comes to the foreground is the nature of devotion in the life of the righteous. Is it possible to serve God without expecting any reward? This Book of Job embodies the faith of Israel and enables us to talk about the nature of God, individual piety, and justice in the world. Most importantly, I hope that the study will clarify for all of us the inner voice of our own spiritual journey.

Discussion and Action

1. The author writes that the Book of Job "straddles the traditions of explosive expressions of song and dance . . . and the sober and restrained reflection of scholars." Mark a spot on the floor that represents the first extreme and another that marks the other extreme. Considering your reading and reflection on the book, where would you place yourself with regard to your view of the book? Be prepared to explain your position.
2. Most people understand the parables of Jesus (such as the Good Samaritan, the Prodigal Son, and the Lost Sheep) to be fictional stories that Jesus told to illustrate a point. The truth was not in the actual incident but in the lesson from the story. Then there are a few people who would insist that each parable told by Jesus had to have literally happened or Jesus would be considered a liar. What is your opinion? Can fictional stories convey truth? With regard to the Book of Job, must the events have literally happened for the story to be true? What does the author say about the biblical understanding of the events of Job?
3. How have you explained the suffering of good people to children? How do you reconcile this within yourself?
4. Job expresses his anger, lashing out at God about his fate. As a group respond to the author's statement: "Often we in the community of faith are uncomfortable with . . . outbursts and outrageous language. We want

people to tone down insults and to refrain from lashing out at God." Do you agree with this statement?
5. Using newsprint or a chalkboard, write down the differences, as described by the writer, between wisdom and lament. Where do we find wisdom and lament? Which genre are you more comfortable with?
6. Is there a place in your congregation where both wisdom and lament can be expressed? Or is one more acceptable than the other?

2

The Wager Between God and the Accuser
Job 1–2

Personal Preparation

1. Focus on the dialogue between God and the Accuser as you read Job 1–2. What is your impression of their dialogue? This chapter speaks of a God who gambles. Is this an understanding you are used to? What is your response to the picture of a God who gambles on humanity? Is this a good bet? Continue your preparation by reading the lesson below.
2. The author describes an Accuser who is a member of the heavenly court, which is not the traditional identity of one whom many call Satan. Who functions as the Accuser in your family? your small group? your church? Is it you? How do you feel when the Accusers in your life speak up?
3. Picture God and the Accuser talking about you? What positive things do you think God would say about you? Write these down in your journal. What might the Accuser say about you? Write these down as well, and bring your comments to the session.
4. Have you ever challenged God? Never? All the time? In what circumstances? What is your comfort level when it comes to challenging God directly?

Suggestions for Sharing and Prayer

- Begin the session by gathering in a circle. Hold hands and sing "Lord, listen to your children praying." Follow with each person offering a single sentence prayer of praise for something that has happened in the past week. If a person does not wish to pray aloud, then she or he should squeeze the hand of the person to her or his left. After a round of praise prayers, offer sentence prayers lamenting difficult situations in personal or community life or in the world at large. Finally, share sentence prayers of petition. Close by again singing "Lord, listen to your children praying."
- If your group enjoys being creative, read Job 1–2 aloud, assigning the parts of Narrator, God, Accuser, Four Messengers, Job, and Job's Wife. Stretch a piece of newsprint along the wall. Hand out colored markers to group members (the Heavenly Council) who are not reading aloud and have them draw a sequence of pictures illustrating the two chapters of scripture.
- Share the things you have written during your preparation for the session regarding what God and the Accuser might say about you before the heavenly court. Acting as advocates for each other, add other things you would say in the defense of group members.
- With each person praying aloud for the person next to them, close with prayers of thanksgiving for those qualities that you celebrate in each group member. The leader may conclude with a prayer praising God for both Advocates and Accusers among God's people. End by singing once more "Lord, listen to your children praying."

Understanding

In Job 1:6-12, the readers find themselves in the middle of a divine throne room where God, the heavenly beings, and the Satan (the Accuser) have gathered. God raises the only item on the agenda for this day and that is to consider the righteousness of his servant Job. God deems him to be the most righteous individual on earth. However, the Accuser has a different view of humanity and of Job. After all, he has come from roaming over the face of the earth and knows humanity up close. The Accuser (in Hebrew *Satan*) believes that all humans are corrupt or corruptible. He has been out in the field, so to speak, and refuses to keep his head in the heavenly clouds. His view of humanity is biting and cynical—everyone has a price and Job is no exception.

In the Accuser's mind, Job behaves in a righteous way because God has protected him and put a fence around him that keeps him from all harm. The Accuser argues that if God takes this fence away, Job will curse God. The Accuser has put the issue in such a way that God cannot back away from this assertion. In the Hebrew the Accuser makes an oath that Job will act in this way and, since God protects all oaths, God cannot retreat from the wager put in this form. The Accuser is also at risk, because if he loses he is open to certain consequences not yet stated in the text.

Although God cannot retreat from the proposal of the Accuser, God does not permit the Accuser to destroy the bone and flesh of Job, namely his life, but all other options are in play. At this point in the narrative, the reader is not told what the Accuser will do. Given the nature of the challenge, the reader cannot be surprised at anything and undoubtedly expects that Job will take a beating. It cannot be by accident that the narrator concludes this section by writing that the Accuser went out from the presence of God (1:12b). Therefore, there is no divine presence in the affliction of Job that follows.

In Job 1:13-22, Job's wealth and family are wiped out. All the signs of his status and well-being are taken away. Job is ruined financially and destroyed emotionally through the loss of his family. The Accuser takes a shot at Job, but Job prevails as God has maintained. The scene ends with the assertion that Job did not charge God with any wrongdoing. Job actually blesses God and thus proves the Accuser wrong in his assertion.

Another Attempt

The reader is brought to the divine throne room once again, and the Accuser presents himself in the same fashion as other members of the court. This represents a slight change from the last visit to the heavenly court. In the first scene, he came by himself. Could this be a sign of a demotion? There is no concealing God's displeasure with the Accuser in these words: "you incited me against him, to destroy him for no reason" (Job 2:3). It appears that the Accuser has failed in his function, lost the wager, and has lost his authority. Job has proven God correct in his assessment.

The Accuser, ever quick on his feet, responds that he did not go far enough in plaguing Job. This time the Accuser says, "Skin for skin." There have been many interpretations of this phrase, including that Job will pay with the outer part of his body to spare the inner part, namely his soul. To my mind, given the circumstance of the wager, the Accuser is bartering his life for Job's life. The interpreter who comes the closest to this interpretation is Edwin Good who correctly understands the words of the Accuser as a self-curse. The meaning then of these words is not "let's see if he flunks. The prosecutor stands to lose the most" (*In Turns of Tempest* 195). Good does not go far enough when he suggests that it is not clear what the Accuser has to lose. I believe it is his life, which would be an explanation for the Accuser's disappearance from the narrative after Job proves him wrong for the second time.

The Accuser, having invoked the self-curse, follows with the assertion that human beings will do what they need to do to survive. The reader knows the result: it's the Accuser's life for Job's life. It is the ultimate gamble. Again he asks God to take action against Job so that he can prove his point. God again limits the power of the Accuser to spare Job's life, but it is clear that God wants no part of Job's demise. The Accuser exploits a fault-line in the universe that requires God to stand behind any oath uttered in a self-curse, a tenet of the Hebraic belief system. In the conclusion of the scene, the Accuser leaves the presence of God. In this shift of responsibility for the affliction of Job, the reader discovers the distance of God from Job's distress. What happens to Job happens beyond God's desire for Job. Good rightly argues that it is not clear what would happen to Job and God should the Accuser be right (195).

God knows the heart and mind of humanity and is again proven right in the assessment of Job. On the one hand, those individuals who believe that God protects the innocent and destroys the wicked will need to rethink their point of view. On the other hand, how does God care for a universe where the Accuser apparently can overturn the equation where the righteous are rewarded and the wicked are punished? The reader discovers a God who believes in humanity as capable of great good but appears to meet circumstances beyond divine control on earth. The reader discovers that it is the personification of evil (the Accuser) who does not believe in humanity. This individual is the Satan of later literature, but in this story represents a heavenly figure that oversteps his bounds. His function was to be a prosecuting attorney to establish the truth about individuals on earth. In this narrative he has come to his own conclusion about humanity (all humanity will respond to calamity by abandoning God) and challenges God on the basis of his belief. The Accuser has overstepped his boundaries and loses the wager and apparently his life.

In these two chapters, unlike in Genesis 3, the culprit for evil is not a human who sins, but exists in the design of the universe that has structural deficiencies. Evil emerges and uses resources in creation to undo God's intended good. The reader knows from this point on that men and women suffer unjustly and without cause. The reader knows of illness and death without reason. How then shall we talk about God in these circumstances? Gustav Gutierrez, the great South American theologian, argues that the book is really about how the believer talks about God, more particularly how we are to talk about God from a specific situation, namely the suffering of the innocent. This question in itself requires lengthy discussion. If it had an easy answer, we would have a relatively short book. What's more, the reader is also reminded that an answer for why people suffer is never given in the Book of Job. Evil happens even in a universe where good is intended; more importantly, evil is not the intent of God.

Now let's return to the question of the genre of the writing posed in the first chapter of this study. Once the reader clearly sees the nature of the wager, it becomes even more apparent that the discussion of the dimensions of human life occurs in metaphor, parable, and story. We are not dealing with a literal wager, but a way of presenting the nature of God and the nature of wickedness. In this setting, a fundamental truth, which emerges from the history of Israel and the life, death, and resurrection of Jesus Christ, is expressed: God goes to great lengths to bet on humanity. While we might not use those terms, we, as believers, embrace the view that God loves us beyond all bounds.

Discussion and Action

1. The author writes, ". . . a fundamental truth, which emerges from the history of Israel and the life, death, and resurrection of Jesus Christ, is expressed: God goes to great lengths to bet on humanity."

    Based on this commentary and on your own reading of the passage, what do you think is meant by this sentence? The author suggests that God will always bet on us, whatever we mean by that. What is your feeling about a God who gambles on us? The phrase "skin for skin" challenges us to think what might have been at stake in this gamble on Job and, by extension, on us as well.

2. Discuss the following questions you considered in your preparation: Have you ever challenged God? Never? All the time? Is the idea of challenging God startling?

3. What is the value of an Accuser and an Advocate in your church? in life? If it feels comfortable for the group, discuss who the Accusers and Advocates are in your congregation's life? Recognizing the value of both—the person who praises and the one who challenges—list specific circumstances that illustrate the point. What is required in your congregation to provide the appropriate forum for both Accusers and Advocates?

4. The author writes: ". . . those individuals who believe that God protects the innocent and destroys the wicked will need to rethink their point of view." How do you react to this statement? What was your view of God's actions in this regard when you were younger? How do you feel now? What is the proper way to approach God?

3

The Voice of Traditional Piety
Job 1–2

Personal Preparation

1. Reread Job 1–2, this time focusing on Job's words. Then read James 1:2-8 and 5:7-11. Make notes in your journal comparing the scriptures to Job's reaction in the face of tribulation.
2. In James 5 we are asked to consider it a joy when trials come our way. Does this seem possible to you? How could one accomplish this?
3. Make a list of people you know who have been models of good behavior in trying circumstances. Also look through newspapers, magazines, or on the Internet, and clip examples of undeserved suffering in the world. Bring these to the session.
4. Pray for group members, especially in the midst of any trials or tribulations they may face this week.

Suggestions for Sharing and Prayer

- ☐ Greet each other as you arrive and open with a prayer for patience and endurance.
- ☐ On newsprint or chalkboard write down proverbs (biblical or otherwise) that seem to suggest that self-denial or suffering will end in a good outcome. (An example might be "Early to bed, early to rise, makes us healthy, wealthy, and wise.") Do you think this is a prevalent world view?

- ☐ Share among group members your lists of those who have been good examples in time of suffering as well as those who have suffered undeservedly. The author calls this chapter "The Voice of Traditional Piety." Based on your reading of the chapter, can you use that voice to speak to those who have suffered undeservedly? Have one group member quote or paraphrase from the examples of the suffering. Have another group member respond with the "voice of traditional piety." Does this seem to be an adequate response?
- ☐ Talk about the hardest day you ever had coming to church? What happened that made you reluctant to come to God and to be with God's people? Were people helpful? Did others know your circumstances? Have you responded to hardship or alienation from God and God's people (your own or someone else's) with the "voice of traditional piety"? If not, how did you respond?
- ☐ Offer sentence prayers of encouragement and grace for each other. Close by singing "Trust and obey."

Understanding

Most of us think of Job as the prime example of the patient one who endures suffering without complaint. This is the view of Job in the first two chapters of the book. However, the figure of the righteous sufferer who does not raise his voice in the event of catastrophe appeared as early as the second millennium B.C. A text was discovered in Sumer that describes such an individual: "You have doled out suffering ever anew. . . . My God, I would stand before you, would speak to you . . . my word is a groan (Pritchard, *Ancient Near Eastern Texts* 590). In the text itself, the individual does not become impatient in his suffering. Because you may not have been aware of this particular tradition, your thinking about suffering without complaint most likely has been associated with the phrase "the patience of Job."

In the New Testament, the writer of James holds up Job as the model for Christian behavior in the face of great suffering (James 5:7ff):

> *Be patient, therefore, beloved, until the coming of the Lord. . . . do not grumble against one another. . . . As an example of suffering and patience, beloved, . . . we call blessed those who showed endurance. You have heard of the endurance of Job.*

James has in mind the Job of the prologue (chapters 1–2), since he writes about avoiding grumbling and enduring patiently. This description hardly applies to the voice of Job in the chapters beyond the prologue. Perhaps James also has Job in mind when he talks about the tongue in chapter 3. A loose tongue contaminates the whole body because it, of all the organs of the body, has the power to direct one's whole being. Our task as believers is to tame the tongue and avoid the deadly poison of impassioned speech.

Job's Piety
Job's piety, at the center of attention in Job 1–2, is more important than his genealogy, his wealth, his standing in the community. The reader knows that Job is "blameless and upright." The Hebrew word *tam*, translated "blameless," has the meaning of completion and integrity. The Hebrew word *yasar*, translated "upright," has the sense of going straight in relationships. Job has integrity with God and lives in right relationship with his neighbors. In addition, "he feared God and turned away from evil" (1:1). Observe the same parallel structure in Proverbs 3:7: "Fear the Lord and turn away from evil," the description of what it means to be righteous. Job fears God with a sense of awe that leads to an appropriate relationship with his neighbor. The writer underscores these characteristics of Job's devotion three times (Job 1:1; 1:8; 2:3).

Job's family, wealth, and social standing reflect this righteous behavior. Job had a model family, seven sons and three daughters. (In the ancient Ugaritic texts, the Canaanite god Baal is blessed with seven sons and three daughters, apparently the perfect divine family.) A model family is the reward for righteousness as the psalmist states: "your children will be like olive shoots around your table. Thus shall the man be blessed who fears the Lord" (Ps. 128:3-4). A man's family reflects the perfection of his character.

Job is described as a righteous man without blemish with a perfect household. In Job 1:5, we see him as the anxious father who is concerned about his children's behavior. The children of Job are party animals and accustomed to celebrating. He worries that in their celebrations they might commit some sin against God. Job begins each day praying on behalf of his children and offers sacrifices to assure their safety. As a devoted father, he rises early every morning to fulfill this self-imposed obligation on behalf of his sons and daughters. Job is the perfect father, caring for his charges in the most meticulous way. His greatest desire for them is that they stand in right relationship with God. The linkage between righteousness and well-being is clear, and the scene ends with the observation, "This is what Job always did," that is, pray and offer sacrifice for others that God may attend to them.

What Will Happen If . . . ?
The real question posed in these first two chapters occurs then in the first gathering before the Lord. What will happen if God takes away the fence that protects Job and his family from all harm? Will Job under these circumstances maintain his loyalty to God? The Accuser believes that Job will turn against God and give up his devotion. God, on the other hand, trusts his servant Job to maintain his piety in all circumstances.

In the first instance, Job is tested by the loss of his family and treasure. In response to this disaster, Job rends his garments and shaves his head in acts of mourning for his children. He then falls to the ground and worships God. The Hebrew word for worship is *shchch*, which expresses the highest form of obeisance to God. In other words, Job ends this day as he has all others—by worshiping God. There is no change in his relationship with the center of his devotion. Job then makes a simple confession: "Naked I came from my mother's womb, and naked shall I return there; . . . blessed be the name of the Lord" (1:21). Job makes a common observation that we all end up with nothing. The use of the phrase "return there" simply refers to the realm of death (this echoes the phrases from Gen. 3:19, "you are dust and to dust you shall return," and Eccl. 12:7, "and the dust returns to the earth"). In Hebrew thought, humanity has a beginning and an end, no more. Each individual ends the way he or she began, with nothing.

Job also attributes both fortune and misfortune to God. The prerogative of God to give and to take he does not dispute. God has the power to build up his family and fortune and has the power to take it away. There is no suggestion in Job's mind that his misfortune stems from another source. Nor does Job dispute the justice or injustice of this action. In this catastrophe he maintains the same level of piety and does not lift his voice against God in what has happened to him.

By the end of chapter 2, Job is plagued with terminal illness, loathsome sores that are incurable. What will Job do now? Will Job fall into cynicism and despair after having been mistreated and now suffering additional agony and heartache? Will he simply mouth pious platitudes about God in a world where evil abides and disrupts? If we had only these two chapters, the answer to the second question would be yes. Job continues with what appears to be the same level of devotion as we observed in the first disaster. However, his response this time is shorter and more clipped in its expression. Job simply says, "Shall we receive the good at the hand of God and not receive the bad?" (Job 2:10). In these chapters Job restrains his tongue and accepts his lot in life with devotion. We end where we began—with the assertion that Job accepts his suffering with patience and continued devotion.

Perhaps his short answer at the end of the prologue derives from the fact that he is extremely ill. He can only care for himself at this point. The writer makes the observation that Job did not sin against God with his lips (2:10). Or could this observation imply that there is a change going on in Job that suggests a completely different attitude or outlook? In the next session, the reader will hear a different voice or voices that define a different form of piety than the traditional view of the first two chapters.

Discussion and Action
1. What do you think of Job's response in chapters 1 and 2? Is he pious? or ridiculous?
2. The author writes, "Job also attributes both fortune and misfortune to God." Do you believe that both fortune and misfortune come from God? Read James 1:13-17 aloud. How does this scripture text speak to the author's statement?
3. The author makes the point that regardless of what Job might have been thinking, he did not sin "with his lips." At this stage in the story he did not speak out against God. Is it enough that we do not speak aloud against God? Should we keep our thoughts to ourselves? Should we share our thoughts with God? with others?
4. If the Book of Job had ended with chapter 2, how would you phrase the moral of the story? How would you feel about such an ending?
5. Who are the suffering in your own community? Can the "voice of traditional piety" speak to them? Under what circumstances? What other voice might be needed?

4

The Voice of a Caring Spouse
Job 2:9

Personal Preparation

1. Read Job 2:9 aloud. Read the verse again in other Bible translations that you may have access to, either in your church or local library or through the Internet.
2. Read Jeremiah 28:1-17. This is the story of a prophet who, in Jeremiah's time, refused to give bad news and chastised Jeremiah for not telling good news (which turned out to be false). In your journal write your answers to the following questions: What comprises true caring—critical or uncritical speech? How does each sort of speech feel at the time tragedy strikes?
3. Job responds sharply to his spouse's statement. In times of stress or tragedy, how have you responded to the statements of others? Would you have responded differently in other circumstances?
4. If you have a Bible dictionary or access to the Internet, look up references to wisdom as it relates to the Bible. Write down one or two definitions that you find.
5. Pray this week for those whose criticism of you, deserved or undeserved, either stung or struck a nerve. Do not pray that these people will change to suit you, but pray instead for God's will to be done for and with these individuals.

Suggestions for Sharing and Prayer

- Welcome one another. After a time of sharing events of the past week, gather seated in a circle. Review the fact that Job 2:9 uses the Hebrew word *barak* (or *brk*), which can mean blessing or curse. Then take a deep and calming breath before sharing Job 2:9 in a *lectio divina* format.
    a. The leader reads the verse aloud, inviting group members to focus on one word or phrase that seems to jump out at them. The leader reads the verse once again, this time substituting the translation "bless" for the word translated as "curse." Group members sit in silence and reflect on the word or phrase and open their hearts to the Spirit of God to speak to them.
    b. After a minute have another individual from the group, usually a member of the opposite sex of the first reader, read the verse aloud twice, using both "bless" and "curse." Again group members listen and pray.
    c. The verse is read aloud by the leader or first reader in the same manner for a fourth and final time.
    d. After a few moments, sing together "Alas, and did my Savior bleed?"
- After taking time to stand and stretch, resume the time of sharing and prayer. Recall times when a caring person has told the truth to you and how you responded to that person at the time—and later.
- The author suggests that although many have looked at Job's spouse in a negative light, she is telling the truth as a caring spouse. When it comes to death and dying, how have group members experienced the difficult truth in this situation?
- Pray sentence prayers for help in honoring difficult truths.

Understanding

The student may wonder how a writer can devote a whole chapter in this study to a person who is given only one verse of speech. Although she is brushed aside as one of the foolish women (v. 10), Job may have taken his wife's words to heart by chapter 3, for hers is the only voice to have suggested such a new direction. Job changes his tone and outlook almost immediately after his wife speaks.

How then shall we explain her reaction? She asks, "Do you still persist in your integrity? Bless (*or* curse) God and die." Her use of the word *integrity* mirrors God's evaluation of Job. She recognizes Job's determination and the incorruptibility of his moral purpose, but she must question within herself, Is it worth it? The second part of her advice permits two separate interpretations. The Hebrew word *brk*, translated in our Bibles as "curse," is the word for "bless." In the Hebrew it would be abhorrent to any writer to use *arr*, the word for "curse," and God in the same sentence. Therefore, many commentators euphemistically translate *brk* to mean curse, which is logical when it comes from the mouth of the Accuser (see 1:11 and 2:5). But coming from Job's wife, *brk* as "curse" is not so obvious. Whether we translate *brk* as "curse" or "bless," the bigger question is how shall we interpret the wife's suggestion to Job to give up?

The early church fathers saw the wife of Job as a temptress and handmaiden of the devil. For example, Augustine had a low view of women, and Job's wife was no exception. In a recent commentary on Job, Norman Habel makes the following observation about Job's wife: "She is clearly not a patient comforter who, like the friends, waits seven days before presenting her ideas. Her function, as Augustine said, is to play the role of *diaboli adjutix,* the Satan's unwitting ally" (*The Book of Job* 96).

Throughout much Christian interpretation, Job's spouse is either intentionally or unintentionally a pawn of the Accuser, intending for Job to curse God and bring his life to an end.

Another Viewpoint
Solomon Freehof, in his commentary, makes the following observation: "Other commentators, not wishing to have Job's wife so easily shaken from her faith, say that . . . 'she said to him since you may not be able to endure the suffering and in your misery you might blaspheme, it is better that you pray to God that you may die while you are still pure and innocent.'" He then cites an early Jewish interpretation of the verse translated thus: "Pray to God that you be allowed to die" (*Book of Job* 51). This view is certainly not ruled out by the text and provides another interpretation of the role of Job's wife.

The reader may be helped by further evidence from the text. What kind of illness does Job face? The reader is told that the Accuser has "inflicted loathsome sores on Job from the sole of his foot to the crown of his head" (2:7b). The word *shechin,* boil or sore, occurs in other texts where someone has sinned against God. In Deuteronomy 28:35, the exact same disease with the same descriptors was threatened against the Israelites when they were disobedient. The disease is untreatable. When the pharaoh rebelled against God, a similar disease befell the Egyptians (Exod. 9:9). The Accuser has perpetrated the cruelest of hoaxes—the most righteous man is cursed with an incurable disease associated with rebellion against God.

I can only speak from my own experience when a good friend of mine was on his deathbed with a terminal illness. I could hardly control myself in the face of his pain. I hoped with all my heart that he would not have to deal with such agony and suffering. I thought, Why prolong life under these circumstances? Job's wife found herself watching someone she cared for who, from her perspective, had no hope of survival. I believe that she spoke out of pity for her husband and a desire to see his suffering end (see Weiss, *The Story of Job's Beginnings* 70).

Before we examine Job's response and the conclusion of this chapter, we should observe the expanded role of the feminine in wisdom literature. In the first nine chapters of Proverbs, the feminine figure of Wisdom stands beside God at the beginning of creation. In Proverbs it is the wise queen who offers advice and council to her son. In the Septuagint, the name applied to the oldest Greek translation of the Hebrew Bible, Job's wife has an expanded speech, sensitive and sympathetic to her husband. In this we see the emerging voice of the feminine that leads to a healthy and full community life.

A Change in Attitude
Job does not interpret his wife's advice as sympathetic to his cause. He calls her a foolish woman. The Hebrew word for foolish implies both intellectual and moral stupidity, in other words, "You idiot!" The snap response may well be the reaction of an individual fighting for his life. His tone has changed from his earlier response in Job 1:13-22. Even Job's statement about God is clipped and to the point: "Shall we receive good at the hand of God and not receive the bad?" (2:10). How he understands the nature of God may be changing even as he chastises his wife.

The scene ends with the observation that Job "did not sin with his lips." In a carefully constructed narrative, the author of Job uses phrases and repetition in all likelihood for us to hear the change from earlier verses. Meir Weiss argues convincingly against a commonly held view that Job's piety remains the same throughout the prologue. To see Job's piety as unchanging would simply place what we read here in a theoretical realm, which does not touch life as it is lived. According to Weiss, "the characterization of the protagonist and his reaction to the world must be built on real human nature" (74). The intervention of the Accuser has changed Job's perspective on the world, and the short phrase "with his lips" suggests a shift in the inner life of Job. If Job had been unaffected by all that happened to him, there would be little for us to respond to. He would be like an automaton who goes through the fires of life unscathed and with no emotional or spiritual consequence. In other words, he would remain outside of our experience and frame of reference.

Job's wife awakens him with her small but telling voice that humanizes him. In that exchange a change occurs, even if it is not recognized by Job at first. This new attitude makes possible the lament of chapter 3. Job's quick response to his wife's comment means that she has struck a raw nerve. The quiescent Job is awakening; he will not be the same again. The words that issue from his lips, given the circumstances of his life, are what we might expect from someone who has suffered so much loss. Without the prodding of a sympathetic wife, Job would be a different book with a different voice than the one we are about to discover in the next chapters.

Discussion and Action

1. On newsprint or a chalkboard, draw cartoons of situations in which you may not have told the complete truth to someone. Draw two balloons, one that includes what you said and the other that includes what you thought at the time.
2. Recount incidents in which advice that seemed bad at first sounded much better in retrospect.
3. Discuss what the author calls "the feminine in wisdom literature," using the definitions of wisdom that you found in a Bible dictionary or Internet search as part of your preparation.
4. Compare Augustine's description of Job's spouse with that of author Bob Neff. How does your image of Job's wife compare to Augustine's?
5. Is it possible to use what the author calls "the voice of a caring spouse" and sound like you're caring? Role-play a longer conversation between Job and his wife, with each one explaining what they mean in the words they direct at each other.
6. The author writes, "I believe that [Job's wife] spoke out of pity for her husband and a desire to see his suffering end." When have you felt that a person had suffered enough? How did you pray in this circumstance? How do you think Job's wife helped Job to reconsider his point of view? Is it easy or even possible to use what is called "the voice of a caring spouse" without hurting another?

5

The Voice of Lament
Job 3

Personal Preparation

1. Read Job 3. In addition, read Psalm 88 and Jeremiah 20:14-18.
2. In your journal write a paragraph that defines the words *despair* and *lament*. Bring this to share with the group.
3. Reflect on times in your life when you have experienced true despair and expressed lament aloud or silently. How much of that experience is still an active part of your life? How has that experience changed your perspective on life, on God, and on the world around you? Was your faith community helpful during these difficult times?
4. Read aloud Job 3:3-4. Whether or not you currently share the strong emotions expressed here by Job, offer to God your own prayer of deep emotion.

Suggestions for Sharing and Prayer

- As you gather take time to greet one another and to share the news of the past week. Begin the session by singing "By the waters."
- How does the author differentiate between complaint and lament? Have you confused the two in your mind in the past? Share with one another, if you can, examples from your life when you have complained to God and to others, and when you have lamented. Talk about times

when you have listened to the complaint and lament of others. How easy or hard is it to hear this different voice? How great is the temptation to attempt to fix rather than hear?
- [ ] Job suggests in 3:11-19 that all are in the same state after death. How does this square with what you learned growing up, or with your general understanding of the Bible? Is this a biblical view, or Job's view?
- [ ] Job's perspective is in the first person. His world has closed in and he does not seem to believe that others can understand his experience. Take time to pray for those who feel truly isolated by their grief and suffering. Close with prayer for those in despair and those who act out of despair.

Understanding

As we study this chapter, it will be helpful to distinguish between a lament and a complaint. When I lament, I simply desire to get something off my chest so that I feel better. I don't expect a response. In my crying I unload my feelings of distress and feel better without any change in my external circumstances.

There are no lament departments in large retail stores. They have complaint departments. When I go to a complaint department and raise a concern, I expect that there will be an appropriate response and the complaint will be answered. The circumstances of the lamenter and the complainer are often the same, but the expectation of the type of response is vastly different. In the complaint I am baring my soul before God with a view that my external circumstances will change, but in lament I am baring my soul before God in the hope of a respectful hearing without a change in my external situation.

The primal laments and complaints of biblical characters can be found throughout the Old Testament. These people ask why they should go on living when life has turned against them. These cries arise out of difficult circumstances as demonstrated in the following illustrations: "Of what use is great wealth," asks Abraham, "when I have no heir?" (Gen. 15:2). "Why should I go on living with this great struggle in my womb?" laments Rebecca in Genesis 25:22 during a difficult pregnancy. After his great victory over the Philistines, Samson cries out in anguish, "Am I now to die of thirst . . . ?" (Judg. 15:18). Claus Westermann observes that this list could go on. In these biblical narratives, the reader sees the laments in their primal setting, in the place where human life appears at wit's end and to which this form of expression belongs (*Lamentations* 90).

The third chapter of Job has many similarities with these situations and two other laments in the Old Testament, Psalm 88 and Jeremiah 20:14-18. The laments of Job, the psalmist, and Jeremiah all have a despondent tone. The plaintive voice of the psalmist believes that God has abandoned him, and he no longer expects a response to his prayers. Jeremiah, after six different prayers, comes to the end of his rope and despises the day of his birth. Likewise, after days of suffering without relief, Job comes to the conclusion that there will be no end to his distress.

Those of us who come from a Christian background assume we are by nature sinful and look first to confession in prayer. However, there is an underlying assumption in many lament psalms in the Old Testament that the one in distress has done nothing wrong. The great Psalms scholar Sigmund Mowinckel observes that there is little room for repentance since the lamenter asserts that he is innocent (*The Psalms in Israel's Worship* 12). In the entire Psalm 88, there is no confession of guilt, only the questioning of the inexplicable lack of response from God; Jeremiah is dumbfounded by God's treatment since he has been faithful to his prophetic task; Job, in his own self-examination, knows of no sin for which he can be held accountable. Not one of these individuals begs for forgiveness. This stance of Job angers his friends because they take the same view as you and I do, that is, to restrain speech and be contrite. Even though we know Job is innocent of any wrongdoing, we as Christians find it difficult to believe that he is without sin.

Job's Lament
Job opens his mouth and curses his birthday. Every Hebrew listener, when they heard the word *curse* must have expected the worst—the cursing of God. Instead, Job turns upon himself and directs his anger to "his day" (that is, his birthday) and not against God. Job despises the time of his conception. He would like to cancel out any memory of what occurred from conception to birth. In this first stanza of Job's lament (3:3-10), the reader is pulled into the intensity by the many metaphors for darkness that swallow up the light of the sun, including its eclipse. The joy of life's beginning is drowned in the sadness that has befallen his life. Thus, the first option for Job is no life at all. In his opinion, he would have been better off had he never been conceived.

In the second stanza of the lament (Job 3:11-19), another option emerges: "Why did I not die at birth?" In these verses Job describes the circumstances of the dead as preferable to the life of the living. Whereas in the first stanza darkness swallows light, in these verses death becomes more attractive than life. In verse 13 the grave is the place where one lies down to rest without any disturbance and sleeps without interruption. There are no nightmares and no discomfort. What we seek in life can only be found in death.

In Job's view, Sheol is the great equalizer. Remember that there is no heaven or hell in the Old Testament since all people, good and bad, end up at the same place—Sheol—the abode of the dead. Among those who have gone to the grave, all signs of rank disappear. Small and great, slave and master, the wicked (the torturer) and the weary (the tortured), prince and stillborn child, prisoner and taskmaster, all share the same fate. No one is in trouble and no on can make trouble. Differences in station, so apparent in life, have disappeared, and conflicts arising out of hierarchy have evaporated. The longing for rectitude in human relationships is satisfied in the darkness of the grave. In addition, you can't take your wealth with you (vv. 14-15). Even those with the greatest power cannot assume that what they build will remain.

Of course, God is the God of the living and not of the dead. God does not reside here. In this domain Job would remain out-

The Voice of Lament

side of God's reach. By the end of the stanza, the reader finds a complete reversal in Job's life. What was formerly defined as well-being in Job 1:1-5 and associated with life has been canceled out by the attractiveness of death. Rank, wealth, family, and relationship with God mean nothing in Job's situation. A short life is a benefit. The life of piety defined by obedience and close relationship with God has disappeared into the Pit of Non-Relationship, Sheol.

The opening of the third stanza (Job 3:20-26) lifts up the two words *light* and *life*, which were enveloped in darkness and death in the first and second stanzas. They are hedged in by "misery" and "the bitter in soul." Since the options of nonexistence and stillbirth have been denied to him, Job must now face the fact that he remains alive. Job does not request God's intervention and relief from pain and suffering. Instead, he retains his desire for death.

Job asks why life is given to one who cannot find the way. In Job 3:23 the hedge erected by God evokes the memory of Job 1:15 where it provides protection. Now it has become an obstacle to seeing what lies ahead. The clarity of life's meaning and purpose has been obscured. One could endure suffering if one understood its direction. Job asks why he should persevere when nothing makes sense. Physical discomfort becomes the focal point of one's existence. In the pain of life, there are no longer third-party references. From this point on in the poem, the first person dominates. The reader encounters Job's pain as "my sighings."

The second dimension of Job's life is fear and dread (v. 25). The words used here do not demonstrate the prayerful reverence contained in the fear of God in chapters 1–2. The term *dread* refers in Deuteronomy to the fear generated by God's anger (Deut. 9:19) and by the threat of disease when Israel disobeys (Deut. 28:60). The Hebrew word *pachad*, translated fear, has the sense of terror as when one awaits death (Sirach 9:13), an enemy (Ps. 64:1), or great evil (Prov. 1:33). Job confronts both physical annihilation and mental terror. Job lives in primal fear.

The third dimension of Job's life is trouble. It comes! There is no ease. There is no quiet. There is no rest. What marked the blessed estate of death in verse 13—sleep, rest, and quiet—have been negated. The reader is greeted with a chorus of no's that cancel out any notion of well-being. Lest we misunderstand the term *trouble* as some kind of mild discomfort, it is the same word that is used to describe the work of the wicked (Job 3:17). The distress and tension of Job's life destroy the possibility of sleep. He has no respite from the continual barrage of the cannon fire of a tragic existence. There is no escape. Job must now explore what all this means.

In the concluding verses of this chapter, the reader sees a sick man who still breathes but does not understand why. Job laments but does not ask for relief from God. In the first chapters, we identify with Job because we want to be like him in his good fortune. In the third chapter, we identify with him because we most likely have felt at one time or another that we have suffered unjustly too. We may also feel that all we can do is get things off our chest, because nothing will really be resolved.

Lament is only one attitude in prayer. In chapter 7 we will explore the attitude of the complainer and the change in Job's outlook in his prayer.

Discussion and Action

1. Read Job 3; Psalm 88; and Jeremiah 20:14-18 aloud a verse at a time, with each group member taking a turn. Each should attempt to read the verse with the "voice of lament," however group members interpret that phrase.
2. Using crayons and sheets of paper, have group members describe the moods of Job, Jeremiah, and the psalmist using different colors. Hang these on the wall for the rest of the session.
3. Is lament a sign of no faith or great faith, or does it have any connection to faith at all?
4. Job had experienced decades of prosperity and happiness compared with a relatively short time of sorrow. If you were a talk show host and Job were your guest, how would you respond to his relative good fortune and short-lived misfortune? What sort of questions would

you ask him? How would you challenge him? To what extent would you sympathize with him?
5. Consider ways in which you and your group can be more attentive to the voice of lament in your community? What agencies exist in your community that you can work through? How is your church set up to hear lament, either personal or corporate, from among members either within or outside of worship? Is the regular worship a time for hearing lament? Can or should lament psalms or passages have a regular place in your worship life?

6

The Voice of Traditional Wisdom
Job 4–5

Personal Preparation

1. Read Job 4–5 in two different translations, comparing them verse by verse. What differences, if any, do you notice between the two versions?
2. Using the Internet, go to www.upperroom.org, and after clicking on the Today's Devotional line, enter October 31, 2002, under Previous Devotionals (on the left side). Print out and read this meditation by Frank Ramirez and bring it to the session.
3. Think about times when you have received or given bad advice. What were the results?
4. Pray for all those, including yourself, who may be in the position of hearing problems and giving advice.

Suggestions for Sharing and Prayer

- After greeting each other and sharing the news of the past week, take time to offer sentence prayers of caring for each member in the group. Sing "Lord, listen to your children praying" as you conclude.
- Define the meaning of what the author calls "the voice of traditional wisdom." Use that voice as you read Job 4–5 aloud, a verse at a time.
- The author suggests that many of us "have taken part in the kind of theological conversation where the participants have staked out a position with no intention to

change, despite the validity of the opposition's argument." What sorts of arguments has your church and/or your group experienced that fit that description? Do you have ground rules for heated arguments, or does your church or group flounder in such discussions?
- ☐ Picture yourself in the upper room between the time when Jesus was crucified and when he was resurrected. Role-play or discuss how you would address the sorrowing disciples, using the voice of traditional wisdom as it pertains to the situation they find themselves in. Demonstrate how the truth of this voice and outlook is proven by the death of their master and the manner in which it occurred.
- ☐ Close with prayer for humility and the ability to hear the suffering of others, and sing "Will you let me be your servant?"

Understanding

The dialogue between Job and his friends reminds one of a dispute rather than a friendly conversation, much like the recorded exchanges between Christian and Jew in the first and second centuries A.D. Name-calling and disregard for the outlook of the opponent were not uncommon in literature of that day. Likewise, many of us today have taken part in this kind of theological conversation where the participants have staked out a position, with no intention to change, despite the validity of the opposition's argument. Consider the disputes between Anabaptist and Lutheran, Catholic and Protestant, Christian and Muslim. In the end, partners talk past one another and develop ever more unyielding positions. Just such a situation occurs in the Book of Job when Eliphaz in chapters 4–5 appears to be sympathetic toward Job and by chapter 22 makes strong accusations against Job.

The speech of Eliphaz in chapters 4–5 gets off to a good start. David Clines maintains that the tone and expression in the speech is supportive. Eliphaz attempts to connect with Job in a friendly and helpful manner:

The Voice of Traditional Wisdom 39

> *If one ventures a word with you, will you be offended?*
> *(4:2)*
> *See, we have searched this out, it is true. Hear and know*
> *it for yourself. (5:27)*

The tone in the speech appears to be deferential, positive, and sympathetic (*Art and Meaning: Rhetoric in the Biblical Literature* 199). These connections are enhanced by the encouragement in 4:6 where Eliphaz asks Job to rely on "the integrity of his ways" and his "fear of God." In this way, according to Clines, "he is essentially affirming Job in speaking without qualification of his piety" (200).

Eliphaz now offers friendly advice. He reminds Job that he has spoken to others in a number of similar circumstances, offered support to the feeble, and propped up those who were stumbling (Job 4:3-4). Eliphaz wants Job to acknowledge the advice that he gave to others in similar circumstances. In this case Eliphaz groups Job with the wise who know what to do. Eliphaz also reminds Job that when the tables are turned, they forget all the sound advice they once gave. Marvin Pope alludes to *The Lady of Andros*, Act II, line 9: "It's quite easy when we're well to give sound advice to a sick man; but, if you are thus, you feel differently" (*The Anchor Bible: Job* 36).

Job is a trained wise man and should understand the nature of his condition through patience and humble acquiescence. In the circles of the wise, Job's outburst in chapter 3 is inappropriate and seems foolish. Job's behavior breaks ranks with the wise. From the friend's point of view, God has created an orderly universe: "Think now, who that was innocent ever perished?" (4:7). This is the way the world is and Job should await this result in quiet confidence.

Eliphaz proceeds to provide a series of arguments that undergird this position. The first argument: the wicked perish (4:8-11). This argument follows his friendly advice and arises out of his observations from daily life. In the parlance of the wise, it has the veracity of scientific truth. Breath and wind (the powers of creation in Gen. 1–2) bring destruction to those who sow iniquity. God oversees the universe so that the disturbers of its sacred order are dismissed.

The second argument (4:12-21) contains what Eliphaz has heard: No mortal can be righteous before God. Eliphaz received these words in the dead of night when he was in deep sleep. In utter darkness and hushed silence, Eliphaz reacted to this presence with absolute dread. The reader is not certain from the text whether this being was God or some unnamed spirit. What is clear in this nightmarish experience is that the God of the friends remains distant, remote, and fearsome. Eliphaz believes from this dream that no one can stand before God and claim that he or she is without blemish. Even the angels fall short of the divine standard. Human beings are frail, live a short time, and fail in the meeting of God's laws. These reflections on the part of Eliphaz can be found in Genesis 3; Psalm 90; and in a portion of Proverbs. Eliphaz embraces these traditions and encourages Job to give up the view that he could be blameless before God.

In the third argument (Job 5:1-7), humans are born to trouble and pain. Eliphaz demonstrates that humanity inherits the problems of its origins, in the sense that it springs from the earth and is cursed by God for its sinful nature. This argument from Eliphaz is based on teaching that can be found in Psalm 90 and Genesis 3. In any event, turmoil is an essential part of being human not just in Job's case, but with many other people as well.

Now Eliphaz provides part two of his friendly advice (5:8-16) and follows a format we all know, "As for me, I would . . ." (v. 8). He doesn't give a call to repentance but asks Job to consider how God restores the lot of the needy, the poor, the mourner, and the lowly. God cares for these people and defends them (Ps. 107:39-43). God does marvelous acts of mercy and sustains the fullness of creation by watering the earth and frustrating the schemes of the wicked. Eliphaz supports his plea for trust in God by an appeal to the nature of God who cares for those in distress.

The fourth argument (Job 5:17-27) states that God reproves those whom he loves. This observation is a distillation of Proverbs 3:11-12b: "My child, do not despise the Lord's discipline . . . for the Lord reproves the one he loves." In other words, Job should embrace his current circumstance as a blessing from God. To react with bitterness denies the reality of God's engagement in the life of Job for his benefit. The wise man responds in obedience to the authority of God without question and accepts with equanimity the hand that he is dealt. This sounds a lot like the voice of traditional piety that we encountered in Job 1–2. To blurt out his feelings as Job has done makes one a disrespectful fool.

At the conclusion of his speech, Eliphaz argues that when the righteous one receives discipline from the hand of God, the land produces, wild animals live in peace, offspring become numerous, and one grows old with full vigor. Life is graced with laughter and the absence of fear. Home and fold are secure as the appropriate discipline of piety is observed. And then Eliphaz concludes where he began with a quiet bit of advice in verse 27: "See, we have searched this out; it is true. Hear, and know it for yourself."

Eliphaz paints with a broad brush rather than with refined and delicate strokes. This speech is more like a conglomerate rock than a faceted gemstone. These globules of argument distill into four distinct thoughts: the innocent do not perish but the wicked do; sin is universal; humanity is born to trouble; and God admonishes those whom he loves. These doctrines of Eliphaz appear to be well reasoned, sensitive, and evenhanded and are the voice of traditional wisdom. However, when Job fails to concur with his judgment about God and the created order, Eliphaz loses patience and accuses Job of the worst sins (see Job 22:5ff.). Thus, hardened theological positions and heated accusations are the outcome of this dialogue. The first of these appears in Job's response. For Job the words of Eliphaz are neither kindly nor diplomatic, but incendiary and provocative. In response to them, Job rises up in protest and complaint, as seen in the next session (Job 6–7).

Discussion and Action

1. The author describes four arguments made by Eliphaz in Job 4–5. Write these four arguments on newsprint or a chalkboard, and as a group define these arguments in a single sentence. Beneath each of the four arguments,

write at least one example from life that seems to prove the truth of that argument and one example that seems to prove it false.
2. Job 5:8-16 describes a God who always takes care of the poor and confounds those who are wrong. Is it your experience that this happens?
3. The author quotes this line from a play: "It's quite easy when we're well to give sound advice to a sick man; but if you are thus, you feel differently." In your experience is this a true statement? or a false statement?
4. Referring to the Ramirez meditation from *The Upper Room* online, which you or some others in the group may have brought to the session, compare the author's point about hearing those who are suffering with the speeches of Eliphaz in this week's passage. To the extent that you agree or disagree with the author, critique Job 4–5.
5. After reading this week's chapter, define what the author means by "the voice of traditional wisdom." Just how useful is the voice of traditional wisdom in the world as you know it? How would you feel if you were addressed in that voice? When have you used that voice with others? To what extent, do you think this is the voice of the church in general and your church in particular?

7

The Voice of Angry Complaint
Job 6–7

Personal Preparation

1. Read Job 6–7; Psalm 55:12-15; and Jeremiah 11:18-20.
2. Many children are told stories about Santa Claus and the Easter bunny that are later proven to be untrue. Job's friends present a world view that may be just as untrue—that good and bad people get what they deserve. What myths or legends were you taught as truth when you were a child that have since proven to be untrue?
3. Revisit the author's definition of the difference between lament and complaint in session 5. If the definition of complaint includes the expectation that the recipient of the complaints will change or change things, how reasonable is it to complain to God? What complaints, if any, do you personally have for God?
4. Are you the sort who complains often, rarely, or somewhere in between? What do you think is the appropriate amount of complaining a person should do? In your experience, does complaint bring results? the desired results?
5. In your reading of this session, note that the author says, "Even God can be named as an enemy." What do you make of that statement? Take a few minutes of quiet to journal on the subject, and then prepare to share these musings with the group if you feel comfortable.

6. Pray for those, including yourself, who have what seem to be legitimate complaints against life, God, or others.

Suggestions for Sharing and Prayer

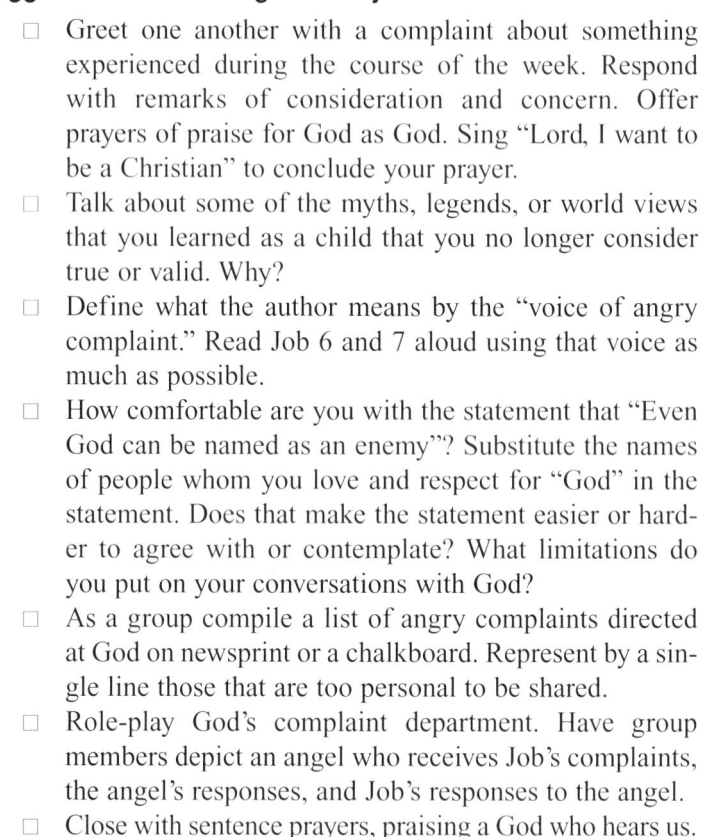

- ☐ Greet one another with a complaint about something experienced during the course of the week. Respond with remarks of consideration and concern. Offer prayers of praise for God as God. Sing "Lord, I want to be a Christian" to conclude your prayer.
- ☐ Talk about some of the myths, legends, or world views that you learned as a child that you no longer consider true or valid. Why?
- ☐ Define what the author means by the "voice of angry complaint." Read Job 6 and 7 aloud using that voice as much as possible.
- ☐ How comfortable are you with the statement that "Even God can be named as an enemy"? Substitute the names of people whom you love and respect for "God" in the statement. Does that make the statement easier or harder to agree with or contemplate? What limitations do you put on your conversations with God?
- ☐ As a group compile a list of angry complaints directed at God on newsprint or a chalkboard. Represent by a single line those that are too personal to be shared.
- ☐ Role-play God's complaint department. Have group members depict an angel who receives Job's complaints, the angel's responses, and Job's responses to the angel.
- ☐ Close with sentence prayers, praising a God who hears us.

Understanding

Job's response to Eliphaz is neither sympathetic nor temperate. He maintains that Eliphaz misunderstands his situation and minimizes his circumstance. Because the world rests on his shoulders, Job complains. If his condition were properly evaluated, its weight would be "heavier than the sand of the sea" (6:3). Therefore, he argues that he has the right to rant and rave and has no desire to be restrained and self-controlled. He acknowledges that he is inconsiderate and wild (his friends' assessment), but, unlike them, he does not find this action to be errant and foolish behavior. Such speech is appropriate to the situation. Job has found the voice of angry complaint.

Beyond the tone of his speech, Job begins finger-pointing, naming enemies who are arrayed against him. He avoided this concept in the first three chapters, but such accusations are not uncommon in the complaint psalms of the Bible. Even God can be named as an enemy. Job hurls this accusation in 6:4: "For the arrows of the Almighty are in me; my spirit drinks their poison; the terrors of God are arrayed against me." I believe the pap and tasteless food in verses 6-7 refer to the advice of Eliphaz, which does not speak to Job's condition and fails to satisfy his deeper need. In addition, the words of the friends do not describe the God Job has experienced.

In the absence of ultimate meaning, Job has no will to live (6:8-13). The reader will note in these verses a shortened form of the request raised in chapter 3. "Let me die" is the cry. The image of a cat toying with a mouse comes to mind. Job has lost his resistance and asks God to finish him off. Nothing matters more than a quick exit. Job has been drained of every resource, and he has no more energy. Undoubtedly, we have noted such a time in a loved one where the will to live disappears like air from a tire. This is not a consideration of suicide, but a request that God end the deeply troubled life.

In Job 6:14-30, Job's energy level rises enough to rail against his friends who have become his enemies. A reading of Psalm 55:12-15 gives a similar understanding of a close confidant betraying a sacred trust, while Jeremiah 11:18ff., describes family and friends turning against Jeremiah, and they are now named as enemies. Job in this section no longer sees his supporters as friends, but enemies.

Job's Expectations
Just as the last section concluded with the loss of internal resources, this section focuses on the loss of external resources,

namely Job's friends. The most common expectation of a friend is that he or she remain faithful in all situations. Job asserts: "Those who withhold kindness from a friend forsake the fear of the Almighty" (6:14). *Hesed*, the Hebrew word for kindness, carries the meaning of steadfast loyalty to a relationship, regardless of circumstance. Job looks for support from his friends and views their advice as an indictment against him. Thus, the reader can understand the charges and countercharges that flow through the rest of the book.

Job compares his friends to wet weather streams, called *wadis* in that region of the world. During the time of the spring rains, these torrents etch the landscape and cleave the rock faces of the desert. In the dry seasons, the traces of these freshets can still be seen and give the appearance of providing a source of water for the thirsty traveler. In reality they are dried up and, instead of life, they bring death (6:18). Job argues that his friends are just like this. When everything was good (family, health, and wealth), they were there for him. Now that the heat has been turned up, they have become empty vessels and provide no balm for his distress (6:21).

Job wants his friends to be in touch with his special circumstance (remember the supposition of the book stated in chapter 1). He is not asking for dishonesty, but fairness, in the consideration of his special condition. In the moment of his distress, he wants understanding, not argument. Even in the sensitivity of the opening words of Eliphaz, Job finds distance and distress. Job wants his friends to see him as he actually is, to turn toward him and look directly at him (6:28-29). A similar sentiment is expressed by Heracles in Sophocles' play *The Women of Trachis*: "Come close to me, stand by your father and look well at my misfortune, see what I suffer. I shall take off the coverings and show you. Look, all of you, do you behold this poor body? Can you see how miserable, how pitiful I am?" (Pope, *Job* 54).

A suffering patient wants sympathy for what ails her or him. "Stand by me" is the frequent refrain. We know this feeling from our own experience.

Job returns to his physical condition (Job 7:1-11). Unlike Babylonian laments, there is scant description of ailments in the complaints of the Bible. In verses 3-5 the reader is provided with a brief description of Job's disease. Job cannot sleep and the night drags on. Those of us who have spent time in the hospital recognize the length of the nights and the loss of rest. One counts the minutes until sunrise. "But the night is long, and I am full of tossing until dawn" (v. 4b). His flesh is torn by worms and just as his skin heals, it breaks open again. No healing is in sight. The loss of rest and the lack of change in his condition heighten his desperation.

Job also generalizes about the hardship of human life. Human effort is like the toil of a slave who grasps a moment to find shade and who lives on the edge until the next paycheck. Life is also like enforced military service with little hope for escape. Job reflects that life is short, a mere wisp of air, like a cloud that vanishes. This observation marks a change in Job's mood. In the beginning of this speech and in chapter 3, Job wants a speedy end. Now he complains that life is too short and he will not have enough time to make his case and complete his complaint.

Why Me?
In the final unit of these chapters (7:12-21), Job opens the discussion with a question: "Am I the Sea, or the Dragon, that you set a guard over me?" In the religious world of Job's day, the Sea and the Serpent (translated Dragon in the NRSV) were challenges to the authority of God. They required continual watching and boundaries to restrain their destructive power. Job muses that he is placed in a similar position that belies his frail status as a human being. This verse introduces the theme of this section: Why does God invest so much time on me, a puny man?

Rest in most settings provides rejuvenation and restoration. Through dreams and visions, patriarchs and prophets received promises and assurances from God. In the cult of Asklepios, the invalid slept in the sanctuary and received dreams of healing at the sacred site. For Job, however, sleep provides no respite because the dreams of the night only frighten him. A good night's rest is denied him and continues his discomfort. Job is left with rattling bones and a pustulant body.

More importantly, the greatest source of comfort is denied him—a caring and just God. Job complains that God will not let him alone. Here Job parodies Psalm 8, which expresses this question: "What are human beings that you make so much of them?" (7:17-18a). In Psalm 8 the answer declares that humanity is seen as the crown of creation and occupies a position of power and exaltation. Job also affirms God's interest in human life, but the answer is not so kind. God's interest in humanity is to test and to condemn. Job cannot swallow apart from the watchful eye of God (7:19). Have you ever had someone watch you chew your food? If you have, you know how unsettling it is. We detest this kind of close observation because that person is in our space. Job relates that God is in his space and has given him no room, not even for the most fundamental functions of life. Job wants to be left out of this intrusive supervision.

Job's complaint addresses the unrelenting presence of God. God has become like the friends, an enemy who watches his every move. If God is caring, God could certainly pardon Job, although Job makes no confession of guilt. This section ends with the perennial why, mentioned three times in 7:20-21a. Job cannot find a reason for his situation. Throughout the book, Job's complaint intensifies so that he eventually demands a hearing that will set the record straight. From this point on, Job expects an answer and an adjudication of his complaint delivered in anger—at least until we uncover another voice of Job in chapters 29-31.

Discussion and Action

1. The scripture text speaks of different kinds of sleep and dreams. What sort of sleep and dreams is Job experiencing? How well do you sleep and what kinds of dreams do you have? Do they vary with your circumstances? How important is it to receive some sort of rest in the midst of trials and tribulation?

2. List some of the questions Job asks in his response to the friends. Are there answers to his questions? Should one answer or should one listen? Do you suppose Job really expected an answer from God or his friends with regard to his repeated question, "Why?"
3. Take a few moments to read Psalm 8, which praises God for the beauty of humanity. Then read Job 7:17-18a again, which seems to parody Psalm 8.
4. The Christian writer C. S. Lewis writes in his novel *Till We Have Faces* that "sometimes God doesn't give an answer. Sometimes God is the answer." What kind of answer can and should we expect in the face of those matters that draw angry complaints from us?

8

The Voice of Judicial Integrity
Job 29–31

Personal Preparation

1. Read Job 29–31; Psalm 22; and Luke 4:14-21.
2. Have you ever been involved in a court case? Were you a plaintiff, a defendant, a juror, a prosecutor, a defense attorney, a judge? What was the outcome of the case? Have you ever been involved in mediation? What was the outcome and what was your part in the process? Did you enter into the process willingly, or were you coerced? Do you believe justice was accomplished?
3. In your journal write a short definition of the "voice of judicial integrity," based on your reading in this session. Bring this to the group.
4. Read Rudyard Kipling's poem "If," found at the end of this session.
5. Pray for those who have been unjustly abandoned by the legal system or are cast out from the confines of their community or church.

Suggestions for Sharing and Prayer

- Greet each other as you gather for the session. Open with prayer, and then sing together "Sweet hour of prayer."
- Read aloud your definitions of the "voice of judicial integrity." Can your group come to a consensus about what this is?

- Job is searching for answers to his situation. What do you think his response would have been if someone had told him of the wager between God and the Accuser? Would he have been outraged, relieved, confounded, confused, or what?
- The author states that Job has "sustained his belief and ethical behavior at the extremes of human behavior, the highest and lowest stations of life." Read Rudyard Kipling's poem "If" aloud. Compare the extremes of human experience, as found in the poem, with Job's experience and consistency of behavior.
- Jesus quoted Psalm 22 from the cross. Compare the themes of abandonment, despair, and vindication found in this psalm and in the Book of Job. Can one use the voice of judicial integrity when reading this psalm?
- The scriptural passage from Luke describes a visit by Jesus to his hometown, in which he gives what many believe to be his vision or mission statement for his ministry. Toward whom is this good news intended? Who will benefit from God's stated mission? Who might feel threatened by this statement? Which side do you and your church stand on?
- Engage in a role play: one group member plays a mediator, and two members play God and Job who meet to work out the present situation without going to court. Others in the group may act as consultants for any of the three parties.
- Conclude with sentence prayers for each other, claiming a place in the ministry of Jesus. Sing "Here I am, Lord."

Understanding

The conversation between Job and his friends collapses in the third round of their exchange in Job 22–27. In chapter 22 Eliphaz accuses Job of the most heinous crimes and worst sins. In the remaining chapters of this section, the arguments become tangled and confused. Many scholars have attempted to rearrange these chapters so the arguments make sense. My own

The Voice of Judicial Integrity

view, however, is that in the end these strong theological positions explode and dialogue ends when angry conversation leads to brutality by each person against the other and the heat of condemnation rises.

After an interlude (the beautiful chapter on wisdom—Job 28), the reader finds a remarkable change in the tone of Job's words. He no longer addresses the friends but appears to place himself in a court of law. For the Hebrew the adjudication of cases occurred in the public square where an individual took up his or her case in the assembly of the elders. One could shift in a free-flowing style from accuser to defendant as the case unfolded in the public arena. Here Job accuses God in more moderate tones, alleging that God has turned against him for no reason or cause (30:18-23). The case is presented in such a way that the reader is invited to join the audience of the court and render judgment at the end of the speech.

In chapter 29 Job remembers the way things used to be, when God watched over him and when his family and wealth were in tact (vv. 2-6). Job held the highest honor in the town and everyone deferred to his judgment. No one spoke until he had spoken; they remained silent in his presence (vv. 7-10, 21-24). Job was without peer in the assembly and without fault. He defended the defenseless and cared for the disabled and destroyed the wicked (vv. 11-20). In these verses we are transported back to the circumstances of the first five verses of the book, but there is greater elaboration on Job's desire to protect the innocent and the weak within the entire community, using his high station in society to execute justice for everyone.

In chapter 30 Job describes his present position not from the ash heap, but as being identical with a social class that has been chased outside the city walls. These people appear to be the criminals who have no residence, but live in caves or lairs like wild animals (vv. 5-8). They must forage for wood for cooking fires and eat roots and leaves of wild plants not normally fit for human fare (vv. 3-4). They are treated like dogs and called disreputable names. Job's honor has disappeared like a cloud, and the deference expected in old age from the young has turned to disgrace. People spit on him; he has lost all social prerogatives and protection (vv. 9-15).

The complaint psalms often depict these reversals, but Job has rephrased his extreme loss not in terms of anger as in Job 3 and 6–7, but calmly and directly—a statement of fact. The reader can feel the tangible change in Job's status and circumstance not so much as a sick man, but as man who has lost all social status. He will complete his case by stating that there has been no internal change in him. The only change is in God's disposition toward him (vv. 16-23), which has left him alone and deserted like some wilderness creature, the ostrich or a jackal (vv. 24-31).

Oaths of Innocence
In the concluding chapter of this lesson (31), Job makes a vow that is framed much the way the oaths of innocence were framed in the Code of Hammurabi, a Babylonian law code written about 1700 B.C. In the absence of witnesses, the accused would take an oath of innocence. A god was invoked in the oath to bring punishment if the assertion by the accused was false (Habel, *The Book of Job* 429ff.). In all, Job gives fourteen affirmations, with only four that list a consequence: "If I have walked with falsehood, . . . then let me sow, and another eat" (vv. 5-8); If I have commited adultery, then let my wife become an adulteress (a paraphrase of vv. 9-10); "If I have withheld anything that the poor desired, . . . then let my shoulder blade fall from my shoulder, and let my arm be broken from its socket" (vv. 16-22); "if I have eaten [the earth's] yield without payment, . . . let thorns grow instead of wheat" (vv. 38-40).

What is most interesting, as one looks over the description of personal behavior in this chapter, is that each affirmation relates to a high ethical standard. Job does not take advantage of the poor and the weak, does not gloat over the demise of his enemies, does not put his trust in wealth, has a high regard for women, has not been intimidated by the crowd, and has maintained his integrity before God in every moment of his life. This level of morality extends to his thoughts as well as his actions. Job's life corresponds to God's assessment in the first chapters: he is "a blameless and upright man who fears God and turns away from evil." Here the reader observes in detail what this means.

Now Job turns and asks that God, his adversary, write the indictment against him so that he can carry it on his shoulder and bind it upon him as a crown. Job would then approach God "like a prince" (vv. 35-37). Interpreters often see these words of Job as arrogant and think that he has committed the worst sin of all, the sin of pride. As contemporary readers, we are tempted to side with the friends and assert that no one can be righteous before God. Thereby Job is condemned for his attitude. But isn't Job simply speaking the truth about his life in the voice of juridical integrity? Has not God made a similar judgment about Job? Is Job required to play the game of humility, even though his words are a simple statement of the facts? Can humanity reach such a standard of morality? These are questions this chapter raises for the reader.

In these texts Job's is the voice of juridical integrity and certitude. In this session the reader discovers an evenhanded description of what Job understands his life to represent. Job has sustained his belief and ethical behavior in the extremes of human existence, the highest and the lowest stations of life. The change in his status has not changed his commitment to God and the ethical dimensions of his life. Moreover, Job refuses to succumb to the prevalent orthodoxy of his day that when disaster strikes one should avoid outbursts of anger and retain the humble voice of traditional piety and wisdom. Job challenges God to explain why God's behavior toward him has changed when Job has not.

According to the understanding of oaths that we established in session 2, Job's oaths require a reply. The reply comes in the "voice from the whirlwind," discussed in our next session.

Discussion and Action

1. Can church members get a fair hearing in the church, or does the church end up providing a judgmental ear to injustice?

2. Job refused to be humble. Do we expect the poor and those in need of our assistance to be humble and grateful rather than angry at the situation they have found themselves in?
3. Job seems to begin to recognize that most people experience life all the time as he has since the disasters, and that for others life is just as meaningless. What does it take for us to identify with the plight of most of humanity? How has the devastation from Hurricane Katrina affected your understanding of the plight of others?
4. To what extent does your study group or the church take up common cause with the poor? Do you blame the poor for their situation? Are you actively involved in changing the circumstances of the poor, such as through community programs that work with the poor in creating new lives, or through Heifer International or other larger programs that work in the world? Is it easier to help the poor far away or in your own community?
5. Does your group or church regularly work with programs to help victims of domestic violence or others who are placed on the margins of society? What ministries do you have with those adults and children who are sexually or physically abused? Is this sort of ministry encouraged or discouraged in your congregation.

If

If you can keep your head when all about you
Are losing theirs and blaming it on you;
If you can trust yourself when all men doubt you,
But make allowance for their doubting too;
If you can wait and not be tired by waiting,
Or, being lied about, don't deal in lies,
Or, being hated, don't give way to hating,
And yet don't look too good, nor talk too wise;

The Voice of Judicial Integrity

If you can dream—and not make dreams your master;
If you can think—and not make thoughts your aim;
If you can meet with triumph and disaster
And treat those two imposters just the same;
If you can bear to hear the truth you've spoken
Twisted by knaves to make a trap for fools,
Or watch the things you gave your life to broken,
And stoop and build 'em up with worn out tools;

If you can make one heap of all your winnings
And risk it on one turn of pitch-and-toss,
And lose, and start again at your beginnings
And never breathe a word about your loss;
If you can force your heart and nerve and sinew
To serve your turn long after they are gone,
And so hold on when there is nothing in you
Except the Will which says to them: "Hold on";

If you can talk with crowds and keep your virtue,
Or walk with kings—nor lose the common touch;
If neither foes nor loving friends can hurt you;
If all men count with you, but none too much;
If you can fill the unforgiving minute
With sixty seconds' worth of distance run—
Yours is the Earth and everything that's in it,
And—which is more—you'll be a Man, my Son!

—Rudyard Kipling

9

The Voice of Creative Presence
Job 38–41

Personal Preparation
1. Read Job 38–41; Psalm 8; and Genesis 32:24-31.
2. Cut out pictures from magazines, newspapers, or Internet sites that depict images from the natural world and the larger universe of your favorite animals, places, and scenes, as well as those places you would like to visit, or have dreamed about even if you know you will never go there. Concentrate on images that evoke wonder in you. Bring these to the session to be included in a collage created during the sharing and prayer time.
3. Borrow a copy of *Horton Hears a Who* by Dr. Seuss from a young friend or family member or your local library. Read the book and bring it to the session.
4. Write a short paragraph in your journal about what you imagine it might be like to meet God.
5. Pray for peace and God's presence in your life.

Suggestions for Sharing and Prayer
☐ The Genesis passage suggests that Jacob is wounded in his encounter with God. God's reply to Job is also powerful. How do you suppose you would feel if you encountered God in this fashion? In what ways have you been wounded by life? Would you say that your experience was an encounter with God?

- If weather permits, take a nature walk outside your meeting place, whether it be rural, urban, or suburban. Read Psalm 8 while you gather outdoors. Also bring back leaves and other items of nature.
- Put together a collage using the natural materials that you just gathered and the images that were brought to the session. Have someone read the Job passage while others work on the collage. What perspectives on God do you discover from the vantage point of natural beauty and wonder?
- List the ways you believe God speaks to us. Which of these have been experienced by members of the group? How did these encounters change or fail to change individuals?
- Close this time of sharing and prayer by praying silently for new and awesome perspectives of God and your world.

Understanding

When I first thought of a title for this chapter, it was "The Voice of Creative Power." This would have been my approach when I taught at the seminary almost thirty years ago. Since then I have changed my mind about the character and purpose of God's speech from out of the whirlwind. Contrary to many interpreters who see God's response as a divine put-down, I see these words as a sign of God's creative and restorative presence in all circumstances. For years I didn't think this speech had anything to do with Job's first reaction, which begged for destruction, uncreation, and the curse of his birthday.

Dr. David Dorsey, professor of Old Testament at the Evangelical School of Theology at Myerstown, Pennsylvania, has shown that there are over thirty nouns and verbs in God's speech that mirror Job's vocabulary in chapter 3. By repetition they appear 140 times. God does not give a rebuttal to each of Job's arguments. That would imply that Job had framed the character of the response. However, the use of vocabulary found in chapter 3 suggests that God has been listening to Job and seeks to respond to his mood of lament and despair. Far from being aloof, God's speech from out of the whirlwind turns Job's vocabulary of destruction into words of creative presence.

Secondly, Job had requested by oath a hearing before God and expressed his desire for God to render judgment against him (29–31). The reader will note that God does not challenge the innocence of Job nor condemn him. As we indicated in the last chapter, the court is free-floating and God enters into this setting with a series of questions rather than a set of accusations: Who is this? Where were you? On what were you . . . ? Have you . . . ? From earlier speeches, Job apparently believed that God would simply overwhelm him and there would be no way in which he could respond. That accusation proves false in the demeanor of God's approach to Job.

Thirdly, God does not put down Job in his summons but calls him a *gibor* (a mighty man or warrior in Hebrew). There are other words for man in Hebrew, *ish* and *enosh*, that denote the weakness and mortality of humanity. These designations are avoided in God's address. This summons is stated twice, "Gird up your loins like a warrior" (38:3 and 40:7). God does not intend to belittle Job as we determined in chapters 1–2. In the heat of argument and accusation, God asks Job to stand up like a mighty warrior and present his case.

Having set the dimensions for Job's response, God does not abrogate his position as the completely Other One who is beyond all human comprehension. God sets out to illustrate this by talking about the universe and asks whether Job was there when the world began (38:4-10). For us today this point is underscored in the entrance to the American Museum of Natural History in New York City, which shows, in the billions of years of the universe, that humanity occupies a minuscule period of time. No matter what your view of creation, the argument brings the same conclusion: God's universe predates our humanity.

To further make a point, God describes God's command over the heavens where lightening, thunder, clouds, sleet, and hail occur: "Have you commanded the morning since your days began . . . so that it might take hold of the earth, and the wicked be shaken out of it?" (38:12-13). "Do you know the ordinances of the heavens?" (38:33). Humanity has a limited perspective of the earth and fails to encompass a view of the heavens, namely the universe. Only God can embrace this totality, which remains beyond human reach.

With the next question, God then moves to the earthly realm (ch. 39), but to a region outside the dominion of humanity. God's description of wildlife extends to lions that threaten life and to animals that cannot be tamed. These animals have avoided human control and live in the wilderness and steppe. The wild goats do not require human intervention to bring forth their young in safety. As soon as they are born, they scamper over the mountainous terrain (vv. 1-4). The wild ox and the onager cannot be coaxed to join the tumult of the city or the security of the manger. They prefer the wilderness that presents danger to humans but sustains their freedom (vv. 5-12). God laughs at the ostrich that disregards the normal parental functions and avoids hunters who seek its plumes (vv. 13-18). The warhorse enters into battle not because of human direction, but because of its innate natural courage, and refuses to turn back from any threat (vv. 19-25). In conclusion, God speaks again of another predator, an eagle or hawk that feeds its young above the sedate, civilized valley with the prey it has found below (vv. 26-30). These animals and birds are noted for their freedom and for their life outside human control.

Gustavo Gutierrez, in his book *On Job*, writes: "All these passages on the animals breathe out an air of freedom, vigor, and independence. God is pleased with creation. . . . Utility is not the primary reason for God's action; the creative breath of God is inspired by beauty and joy. Job is invited to sing with Yahweh the wonders of creation—without forgetting that the source of it all is the free and gratuitous love of God" (75). All life does not come under human control. These chapters are a reminder that God's thought and action cannot be reduced to a human-centered world that is tightly controlled by the limits of human thought.

Chapters 40 and 41 describe two animals, Behemoth and Leviathan, the hippopotamus and the crocodile, two of humanity's most dangerous foes. They represent an unbridled power that lies beyond human ability to subdue. These two animals are a reminder that not all of our life can be brought under our moral domain. There is the tragic in human existence that disrupts and breaks. Carol Newsom concludes her investigation of these chapters with this observation, "Just as the acknowledgment of the tragic structure of existence point to the limits of human self-sufficiency, so conversely does it point to the preciousness of being—but this time in the mode of a gift" (*The Book of Job: A Contest of Moral Imaginations* 256). Just as chapters 38 and 39 stand in contrast to Psalm 104, these chapters stand in contrast to the taming of chaos in the creation stories and also Psalms 93–100, where the seas and torrents are brought under control. The Book of Job then is a reminder of the lack of direct correlation between suffering and the moral bearing of the sufferer, for example, the tsunami or hurricane disasters of recent memory.

How then shall we understand this final speech of God? In his present state, Job describes himself as a brother of jackals and a companion of ostriches (30:29), animals of the uninhabited and dangerous terrain that are embraced in God's speeches. The friends, on the other hand, place God within the ordered, civilized space of urban life. However, at the point of dispossession and upheaval, in the tragic moments of life, just where Job finds himself in this book, God appears with the voice of creative presence that calls to this broken humanity: "Mighty warrior, gird up your loins." While the friends cannot see God in the disordered and disruptive moments of the world, Job does see the creative presence of God precisely in the tragic moments of loss and terminal illness.

Discussion and Action

1. The children's book *Horton Hears a Who* demonstrates the difficulty of getting others to share a belief in something that is clearly experienced but not seen. Using the book as a beginning for discussion, share clear experiences you have had and the difficulty or ease you have had in getting others to believe you.

2. How do we help others to experience or hear God based on the witness from another? Can Job's experience, which is powerfully his, speak to us?
3. How can you tell if someone is truly listening to you? What signs or signals do you look for? In this passage, God speaks to Job. Job listens. What does God have to do to get your attention so you will listen? What do other people—peers, children, and others—have to do to get your attention so you will listen? What signals do you give others that you are sincerely listening to them?
4. In the series of books known as *The Narnia Chronicles*, God is presented as a lion. When some demand proof of the lion's existence, they are told that it is out of the question to command an appearance, for, after all, this is not a tame lion. Do you, your group, or your church consider God a tame God? Do we expect God to confirm our way of life and our beliefs?
5. If you have experienced nature as untamed, through fire or flood or other phenomena, describe the circumstances. Did you learn anything about God in the experience, either at the time or in light of this week's chapter?

10

The Voice of Renewed Life
Job 42

Personal Preparation

1. Read Job 42 and 2 Samuel 6. If you have access to a commentary, such as Carol Newsom's commentary on Job (volume 4 of the *New Interpreter's Bible*), write down a list of the various ways Job 42:6 can be translated.
2. If you have access to the Internet, go to http://photojournal.jpl.nasa.gov/jpeg/PIA05547.jpg to find the photograph of Earth as taken from Mars and print it out for the benefit of others.
3. In your journal write a definition of "the voice of renewed life" based on your reading of this chapter.
4. Take some quiet time to pray and reflect on group members as well as others who may be dependent on you for prayer and ministry. Offer special prayers on behalf of those whom you consider to be your enemies.

Suggestions for Sharing and Prayer

- As you meet, greet one another and thank each other for the opportunity to study the Book of Job together. Sing "Low in the grave he lay."
- What does the "voice of renewed life" sound like? Have you ever heard that voice from others? Have you heard it coming from your own life? Do churches encourage or discourage this voice from being raised?

- The author writes, "What we discover in this journey through the Book of Job is a devotion not built on rewards, but on the recognition of God's free gift to us." Many churches speak of salvation by grace. Has it been your experience that grace is extended by members and experienced by members? Have you acted as if you believe in a God who can be controlled through what is described as the "give me and I will give to you mentality"? What will it mean for you to reject dust and ashes in your relationship with God? What voice do you think you and group members will use in the future?
- "Job is now invited to pray for people whom he has seen as his worst enemies." Take time to offer sentence prayers for those who might be considered your worst enemies.
- Take two minutes to silently reflect on this ten-week study, ending with silent prayer. Then offer prayers of thanks and blessings on one another as you conclude your weeks of study together.

Understanding

After God's first speech from the whirlwind (Job 38–39), Job gave a clipped and abbreviated response: "See, I am of small account; what shall I answer you?" (Job 40:4). In Job's second response (Job 42:1-6), he elaborates by saying that God can "do all things, and no purpose of [God's] can be thwarted." After quoting God's words, Job confesses that he has uttered what he did not understand and discovered wonderful things that he did not know (42:3). Job then responds by again quoting God's words to him: "I will question you, and you shall declare to me" (see 38:3 and 40:7). Then Job says that he no longer depends on hearing about God but that he has seen God in a direct way with his eyes (42:5).

Remember the dream of Eliphaz in chapter 4 where the Divine is presented as a shadow disrupting a night's sleep? By contrast, Job has seen God up close in a much more direct way than his friends have ever seen. Unlike in the first two chapters where Job's response moves from eloquent confession to clipped speech, Job grows in his perception of God and the world in these final chapters of the book. His horizon is expanding rather than narrowing.

Traditional translations make verse 6 the most difficult to interpret: "Therefore I despise myself and repent in dust and ashes." First, this translation of verse 6 runs counter to God's request for Job to "gird up his loins like a warrior" in 38:3 and 40:7. In other words, stop the groveling. Secondly, from the speech from the whirlwind, Job has an expanded view of God's creative power. Thirdly, Job has already been on a heap of dust and ashes. So, does this response simply mean more groveling on Job's part? The answer is no. There is another translation suggested by the Hebrew text: "Therefore, I retract [my case] and repent of dust and ashes." Norman Habel defends this translation, which has been supported by a number of other scholars (*The Book of Job* 575ff.). Job has formulated a case against God, based on inadequate understanding (see vv. 2-5), and therefore he drops his case. More importantly, Job has discovered God's creative presence, which brings an end to his complaint and remorse. As the reader shall see, this is corroborated by what happens in 42:7ff.

My affirmation of this perspective derives from the work of one who has experienced the suffering and oppression in the cultures of Latin America. Gustavo Gutierrez, in his book *On Job: God-Talk and the Suffering of the Innocent,* writes: "Job is rejecting the attitude of lamentation that has been his until now. The speeches of God have shown him that this attitude is not justified. He does not repent or retract what he has hitherto said, but he now sees clearly that he cannot go on complaining. This means that in his final reply what Job is expressing is not contrition but a renunciation of his lamentation and dejected outlook" (87).

Job also overcomes his attitude that God owes him something because of his own righteousness. God is trapped by Job's own view of justice, giving in order that God gives something back. Gutierrez writes, "Certain emphases in his protest had been due to the doctrine of retribution. . . . Now that the Lord has overthrown that doctrine. . . . Job realizes that he has been speaking of God in a way that implied God was a prisoner of a particular way of understanding justice. It is this whole outlook that Job says he is now abandoning. Only when we have come to realize that God's love is freely bestowed do we enter fully and definitively into the presence of the God of faith" (87).

What we discover in this journey through the Book of Job is a devotion not built on rewards, but on the recognition of God's free gift to us. There is no way that we can gain a hold on God and remove God's freedom in his love and care of us. Again Gutierrez writes: "The Lord is not prisoner of the 'give me and I will give to you' mentality. Nothing, no human work however valuable, merits grace, for if it did, grace would cease to be grace. This is the heart of the message of the Book of Job" (88ff.). Devotion is found in the desire for God and a refusal to bind God to a set of principles that the believer defines and controls. God is beyond such a system; otherwise God would not be God.

This outlook can now be substantiated by what happens in Job 42:7ff. God confronts the friends and tells them that they have not spoken correctly as Job has. What has been incorrect in the assertions of the friends? In the end they assumed that Job or his family had done something wrong, otherwise Job would not be suffering in this way. The reader has known from the beginning that Job has done nothing wrong. Furthermore, the friends insist that a person in these circumstances cannot raise a complaint or a lament before God. The only appropriate response is for contrition and humility in order to win God's approval. These attitudes prove incorrect. God requests that the friends go to Job in order that he may restore their relationship with God. What irony!

Job is now invited to pray for people whom he has seen as his worst enemies. The reader is simply told that Job interceded on behalf of his former friends. Afterwards, Eliphaz, Bildad, and Zophar are all restored in fellowship both with Job and with God. Job has learned the lesson of the whirlwind because his complaint is transformed into reconciling mediation. In the opening verses of the book, Job prays for his children. His prayer is now extended to include the larger family of humanity. In his discovery of the creative presence of God, even before any restoration, Job has the capacity to transform life. Life is not devoid of tragedy, but even in these circumstances it is not devoid of the creative presence of God who moves to restore life. More importantly, when one discovers this transforming presence as free gift, one is able to move toward others in the same way. God's free gift to Job results in his act of reconciliation freely given to his former enemies.

The Book of Job rightly recognizes that restoration occurs in reconciliation: "And the Lord restored the fortunes of Job when he prayed for his friends; and the Lord gave Job twice as much as he had before" (42:10). One way to interpret this restoration at the end is to say the friends were right—the just will be rewarded if they wait in patience. My view is that Job comes to restoration by his ultimate trust in God without insisting that God must recognize his goodness and give him his due. Job believes his relationship with God is a free gift, and in that belief he discovers the voice of devotion.

Discussion and Action

1. Read Job 42. The author quotes Gutierrez in saying "Job is rejecting the attitude of lamentation that has been his until now." How do you respond to this statement? How does it compare to previous interpretations you may have had of this scripture text? Is it possible to reject an attitude of lamentation after a period of great loss and suffering?
2. Gustavo Gutierrez speaks of two attitudes of Job's that have been directly changed by his experience with God. What are they? To what extent are they your experiences as well?
3. In the scripture passage from 2 Samuel 6, we read that King David was directly responsible for the death of Uzzah, who touched the ark of the covenant and died, because King David neglected to transport the ark in the proper fashion. A close reading of the text reveals the five stages of grief that David endures until he feels forgiven for the event. What seems to annoy his spouse Michal is that King David acts like he's forgiven. What limitations

do we put on people—and ourselves—after we claim that forgiveness has taken place? What limitations do you suppose others put on Job after his experience of loss?
4. How can you say or not say that you too have seen God with your own eyes? Is reconciliation and restoration a part of your experience in church life or personal life? Why or why not?
5. Share the photograph of Earth taken from Mars. Try to see every earthshaking event, personal and corporate, every triumph and tragedy, all that has ever happened and all that will happen, from this perspective. How does this affect your view of world events? of your life? Does this increase or decrease your appreciation of the grace spoken of in this chapter and the activity of God with the suffering?

Bibliography

Clines, David J. A. *Art and Meaning: Rhetoric in the Biblical Literature.* Sheffield Academic Press, 1982.

Freehof, Solomon. *Book of Job: A Commentary in the Jewish Commentary for Bible Readers.* New York: Union of American Hebrew Congregations, 1958.

Good, Edwin M. *In Turns of Tempest: A Reading of Job, with a translation.* Palo Alto: Stanford University Press, 1990.

Gutierrez, Gustav. *On Job: God-Talk and the Suffering of the Innocent.* Maryknoll, N.Y.: Orbis Books, 1987.

Habel, Norman C. *The Book of Job: A Commentary* (Old Testament Library). Louisville: Westminster John Knox Press, 1985.

Mowinckel, Sigmund. *The Psalms in Israel's Worship*, Vol. II. Nashville: Abingdon Press, 1962.

New Interpreter's Bible: 1 & 2 Maccabees, Job, Psalms (Vol. 4). Nashville: Abingdon, Press, 1996.

Newsom, Carol. *The Book of Job: A Contest of Moral Imaginations.* New York: Oxford University Press, 2003.

Pope, Marvin. *Job* (Anchor Bible). Doubleday, 1965, rev.

Pritchard, James Bennett, ed. *Ancient Near Eastern Texts.* Princeton, N.J.: Princeton University Press, 1969.

Weiss, Meir. *The Story of Job's Beginning: Job 1–2, A Literary Analysis*. Magnes Press, Hebrew University of Jerusalem, 1983.

Westermann, Claus. *Lamentations: Issues and Interpretation*. Minneapolis: Augsburg Fortress, 1994.

Other Covenant Bible Studies

1 Corinthians: The Community Struggles .... Inhauser
Abundant Living: Wellness from a Biblical Perspective ... Rosenberger
Biblical Imagery for God .... Bucher
Covenant People .... Heckman/Gibble
Daniel .... Ramirez
Ephesians: Reconciled in Christ .... Ritchey Martin
Esther. .... Roop
Gospel of Mark, The .... Ramirez
Hymns and Songs of the Bible .... Parrott
In the Beginning .... Kuroiwa
James: Faith in Action .... Young
Jeremiah .... Kinzie
Jonah: God's Global Reach .... Bowser
Life of David, The .... Fourman
Lord's Prayer, The .... Rosenberger
Love and Justice .... O'Diam
Many Cultures, One in Christ .... Garber, ed.
Mystery and Glory in John's Gospel .... Fry
Parables of Matthew .... Davis
Paul's Prison Letters .... Bynum
Presence and Power .... Dell
Prophecy of Amos and Hosea, The .... Bucher
Psalms .... J. D. Bowman
Real Families: From Patriarchs to Prime Time .... Dubble
Revelation: Hope for the World in Troubled Times .... Lowery
Romans: Church at the Crossroads .... Wiles
Sermon on the Mount .... R. Bowman
Side by Side: Interpreting Dual Stories in the Bible .... Ramirez
Spirituality of Compassion: Studies in Luke .... Finney/Martin
Uncovering Racism .... Reid/Reid
When God Calls. .... Jessup
Wisdom .... C. Bowman

Each book is $6.95 plus shipping and handling. For a full description of each title, ask for a free catalog of these and other Brethren Press titles. Major credit cards accepted. Prices subject to change. Regular Customer Service hours are Monday through Friday, 8 a.m. to 5 p.m. CT.

Brethren Press • 1451 Dundee Avenue • Elgin, Illinois 60120
Phone: 800-441-3712 Fax: 800-667-8188
e-mail: brethrenpress_gb@brethren.org
www.brethrenpress.com